Giant Panda or Red Panda?

A Compare and Contrast Book
by Chris Schmitz

Giant pandas and red pandas are mammals. Like all mammals, they share some common features.

Mammals have a backbone (spine).

Mammals have fur or hair.

Baby mammals drink milk from their mothers.

Mammals make their own body heat (warm-blooded).

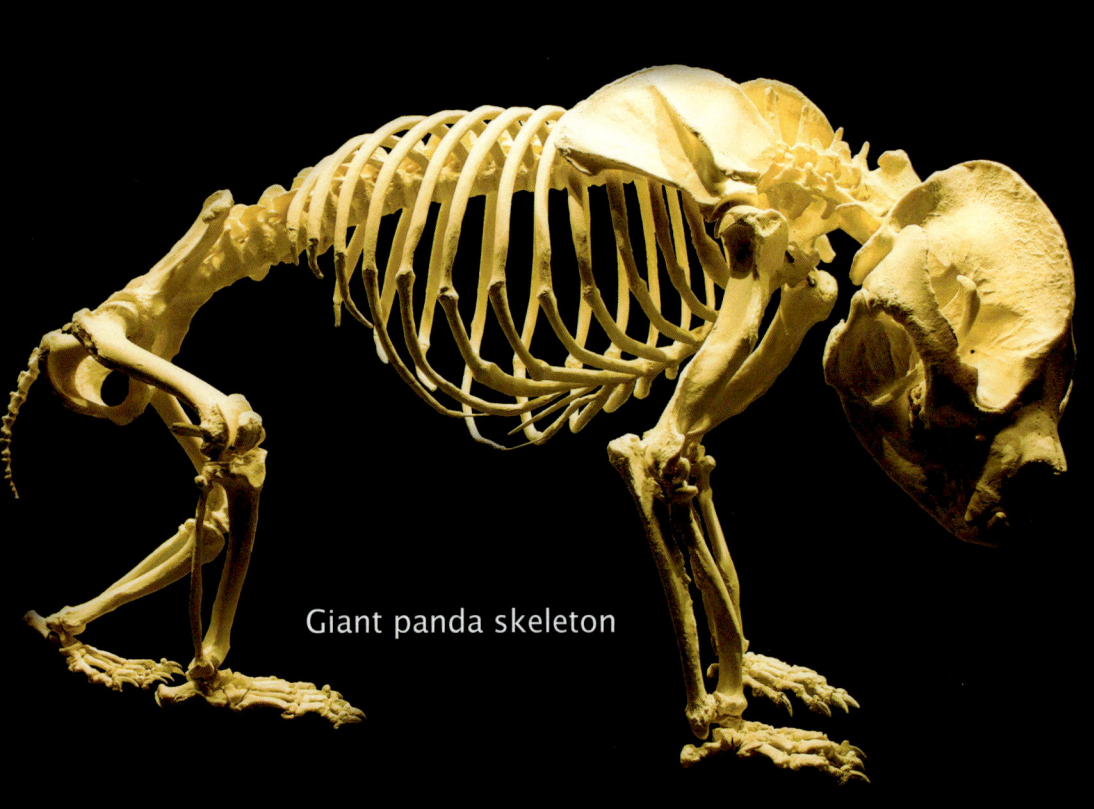

Giant panda skeleton

Giant panda cub drinking milk

Giant pandas are sometimes called panda bears. They do belong to the bear family Ursidae.

Like most bears, giant pandas have big bodies with short legs, rounded ears, thick fur, and tiny tails. They walk on the soles of their entire feet.

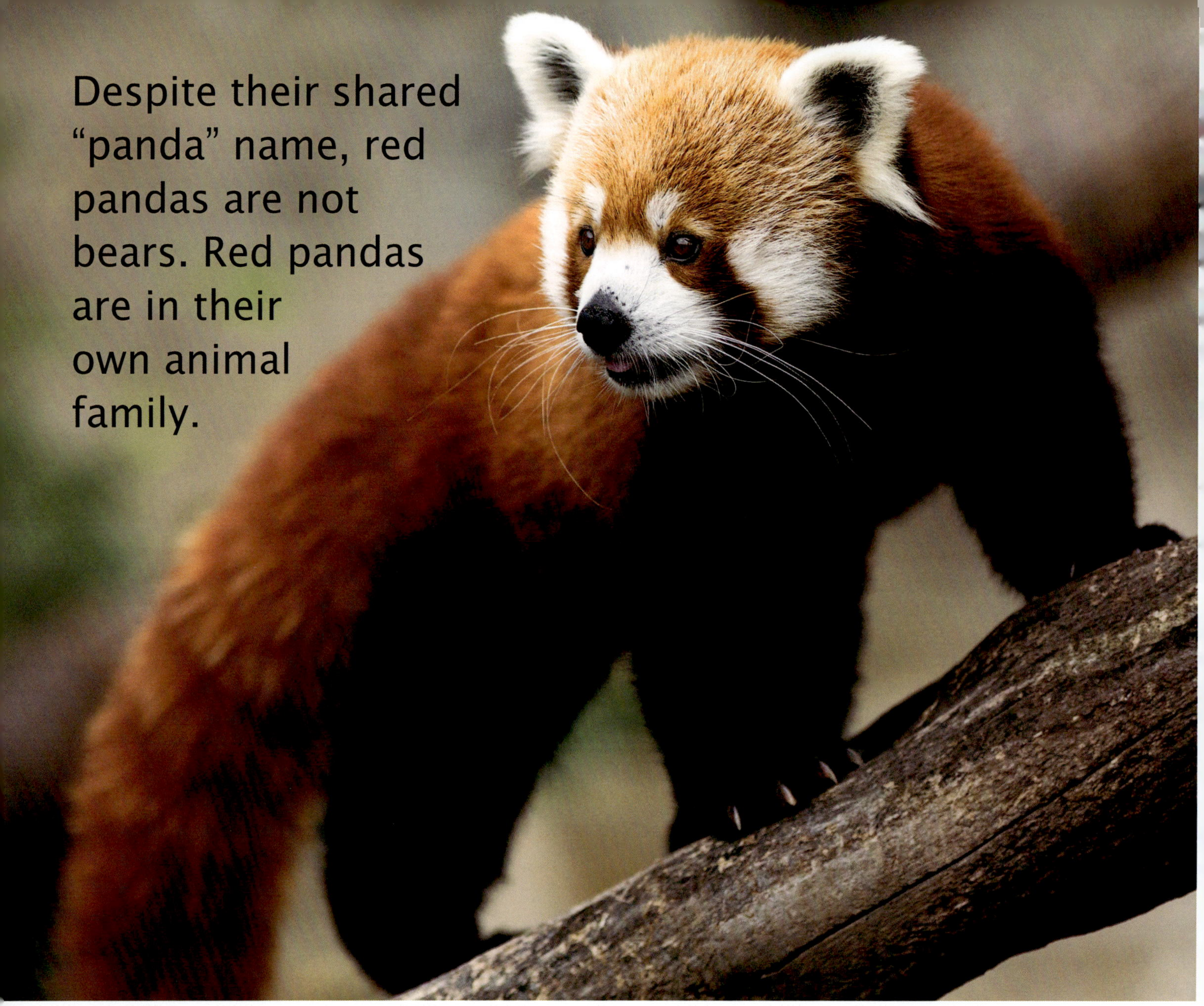

Despite their shared "panda" name, red pandas are not bears. Red pandas are in their own animal family.

Skunks and raccoons are distant "cousins" to red pandas.

skunk

raccoon

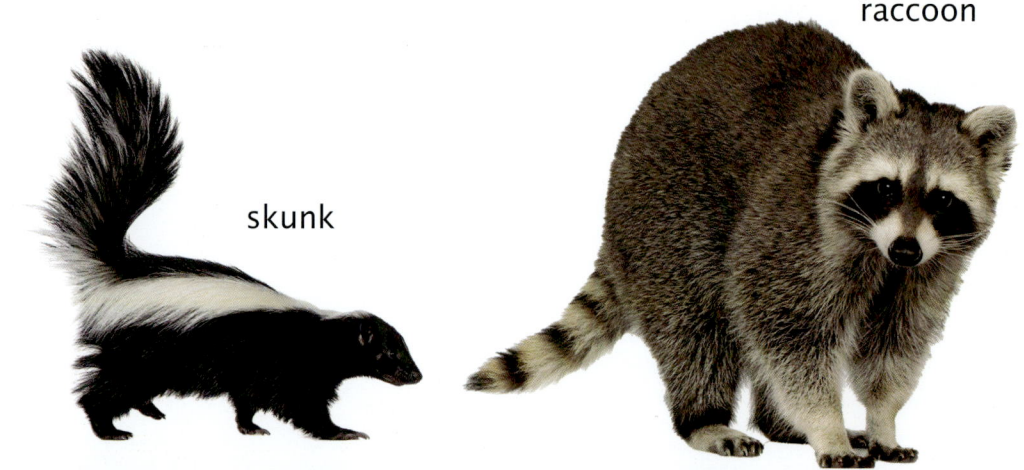

Red pandas are about the size of a domestic cat or raccoon.

They have red-orange, woolly fur with a dark brown belly.

Their faces have red-orange "tear tracks" running down both cheeks.

Their long furry tails have tan and red stripes and are used for balance.

Both pandas eat bamboo as their main diet. They must eat a lot of bamboo because they only digest 20-30% of what they eat.

A hungry giant panda may spend 16 hours a day eating up to 80 pounds of bamboo.

A red panda can spend up to 13 hours a day looking for and eating as many as 20,000 bamboo leaves!

Both pandas need to eat all winter long. They rely on their thick fur to keep warm.

Red pandas curl up with their tails covering their noses to keep warm.

Both pandas have five finger-digits like us.

They also have a special wrist bone that acts like a thumb (pseudothumb). They curl their digits towards the wrist thumb to hold onto bamboo and other things.

Both pandas have long claws to help them climb trees and protect themselves.

While cats can fully retract their claws, red pandas can partly pull their claws in and out (semi-retractable). They can even turn their ankles around to go down tree trunks headfirst!

red panda's rotated ankle

red panda's retracted claws

Although giant pandas spend most of their time on the ground, they are excellent climbers and swimmers.

Red pandas spend most of their time in trees, even when they sleep.